The Cities Coloring

Coloring Book of The Cities For Adults

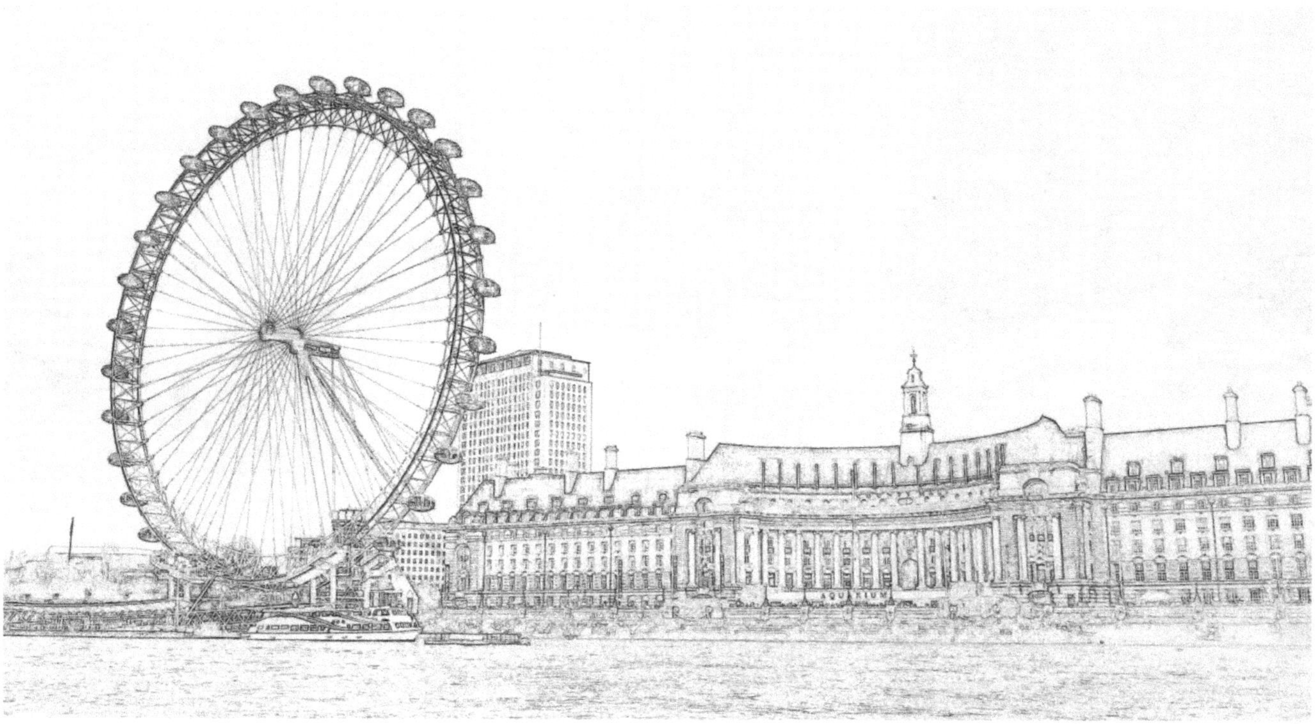

Catherine Johnson

The Cities Coloring

Coloring Book of The Cities For Adults

ISBN-13: 978-1539915973

ISBN-10: 1539915972

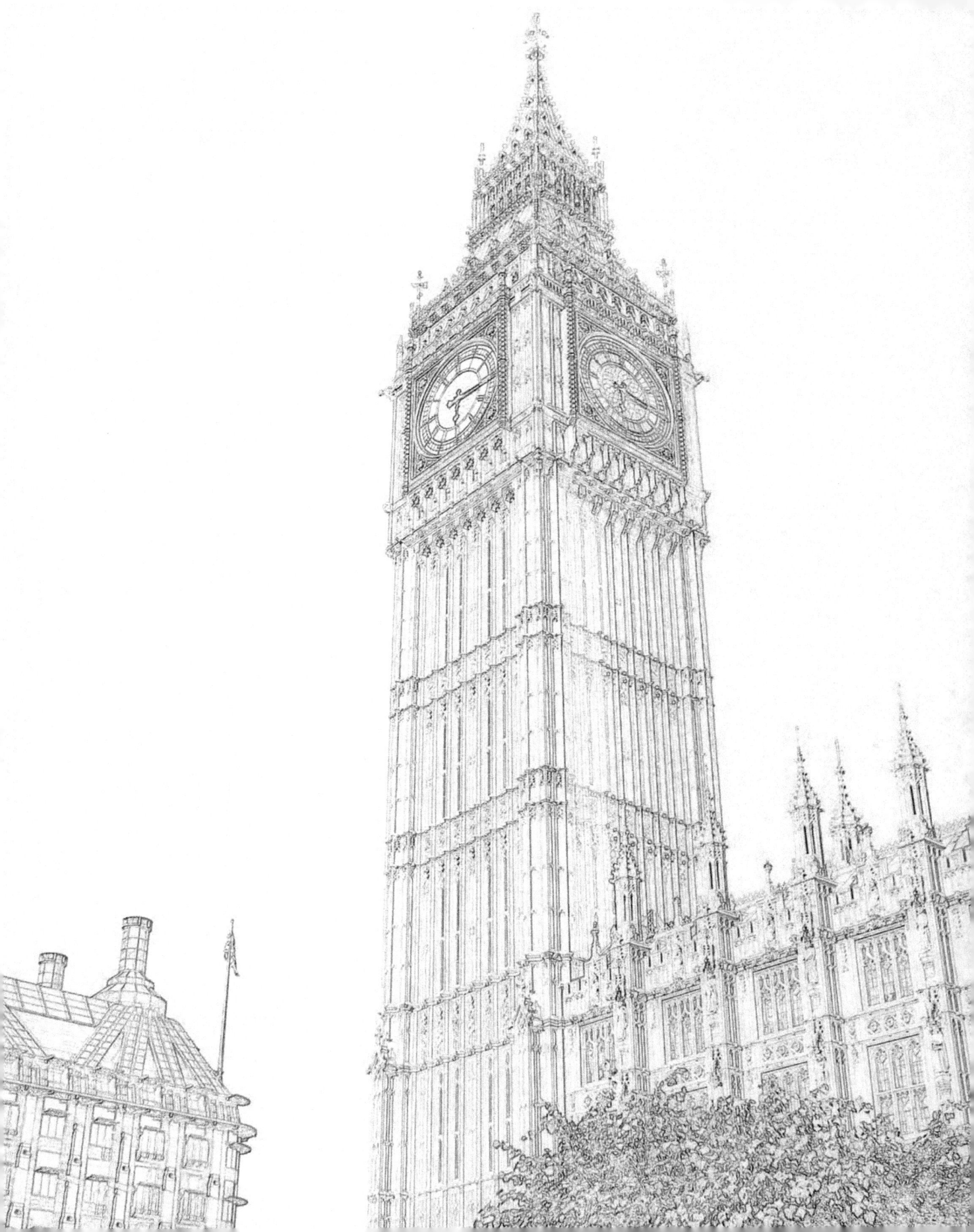

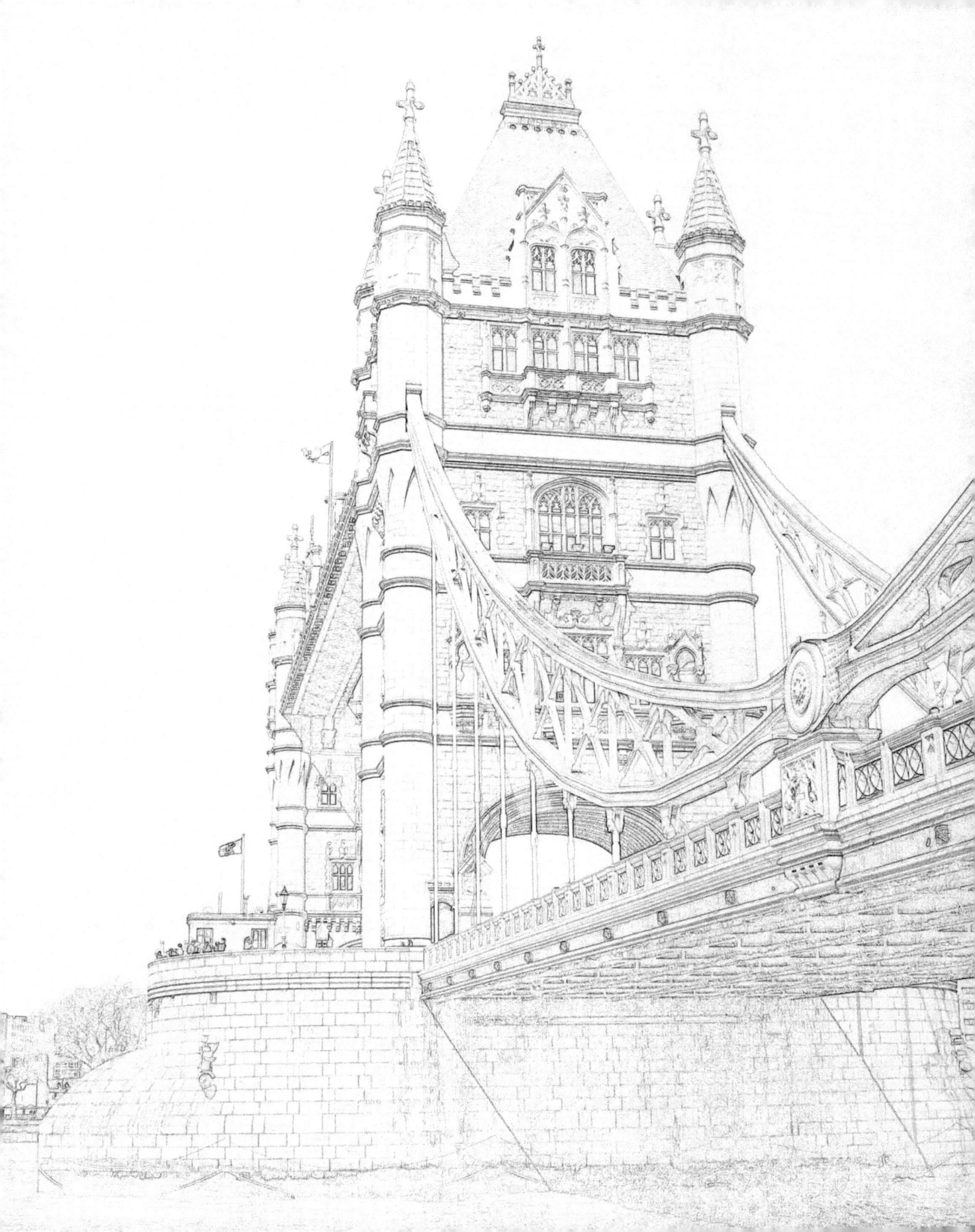

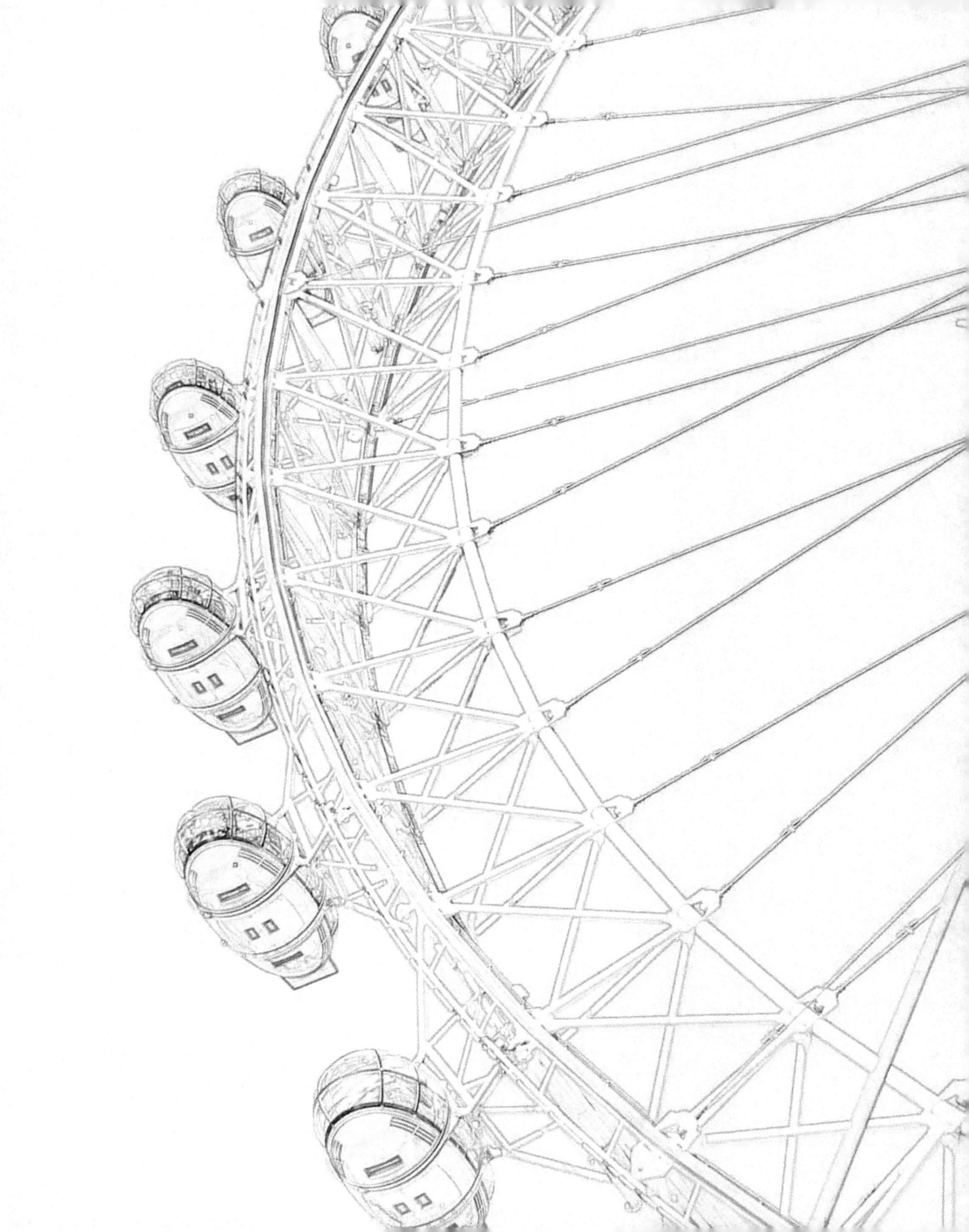

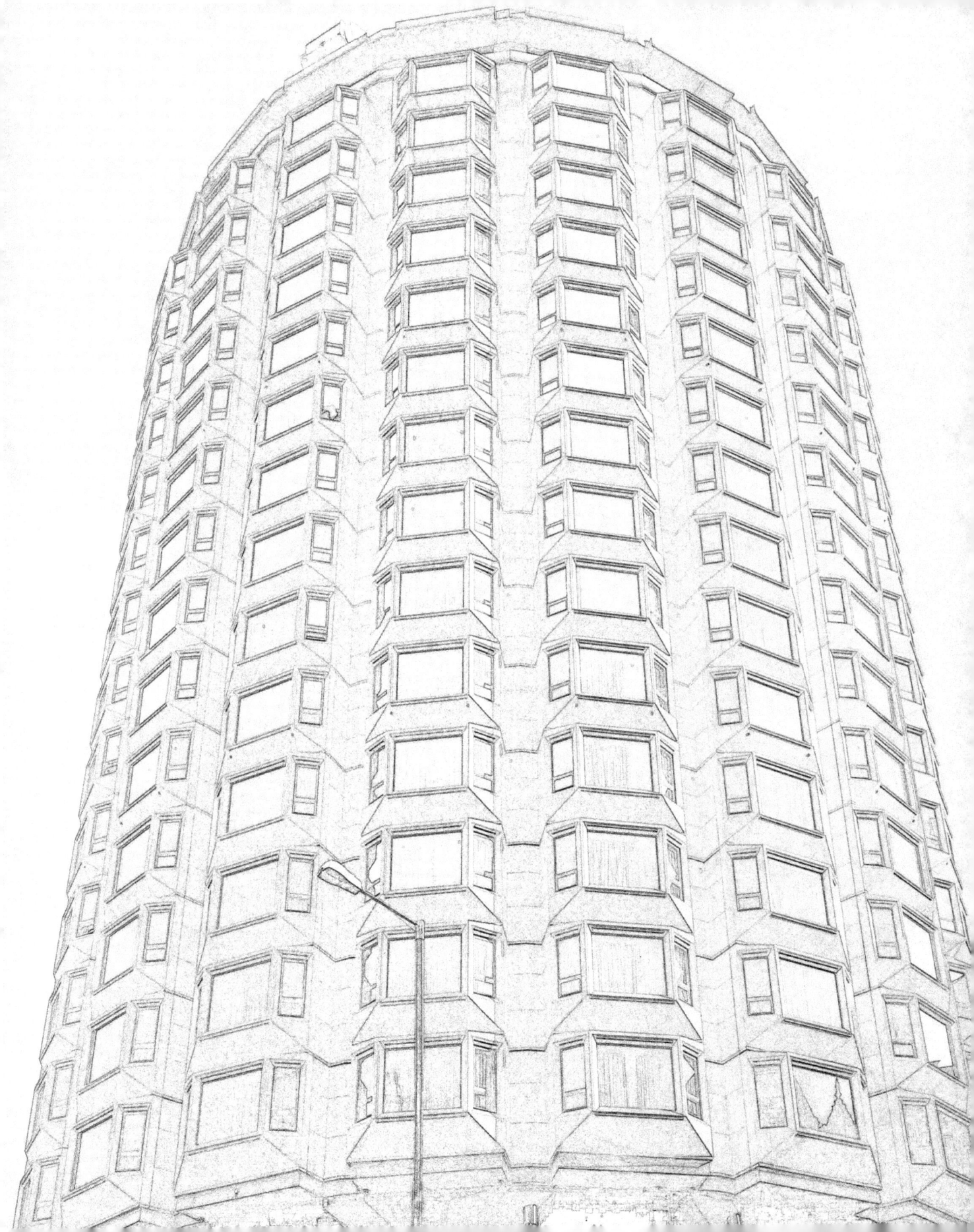

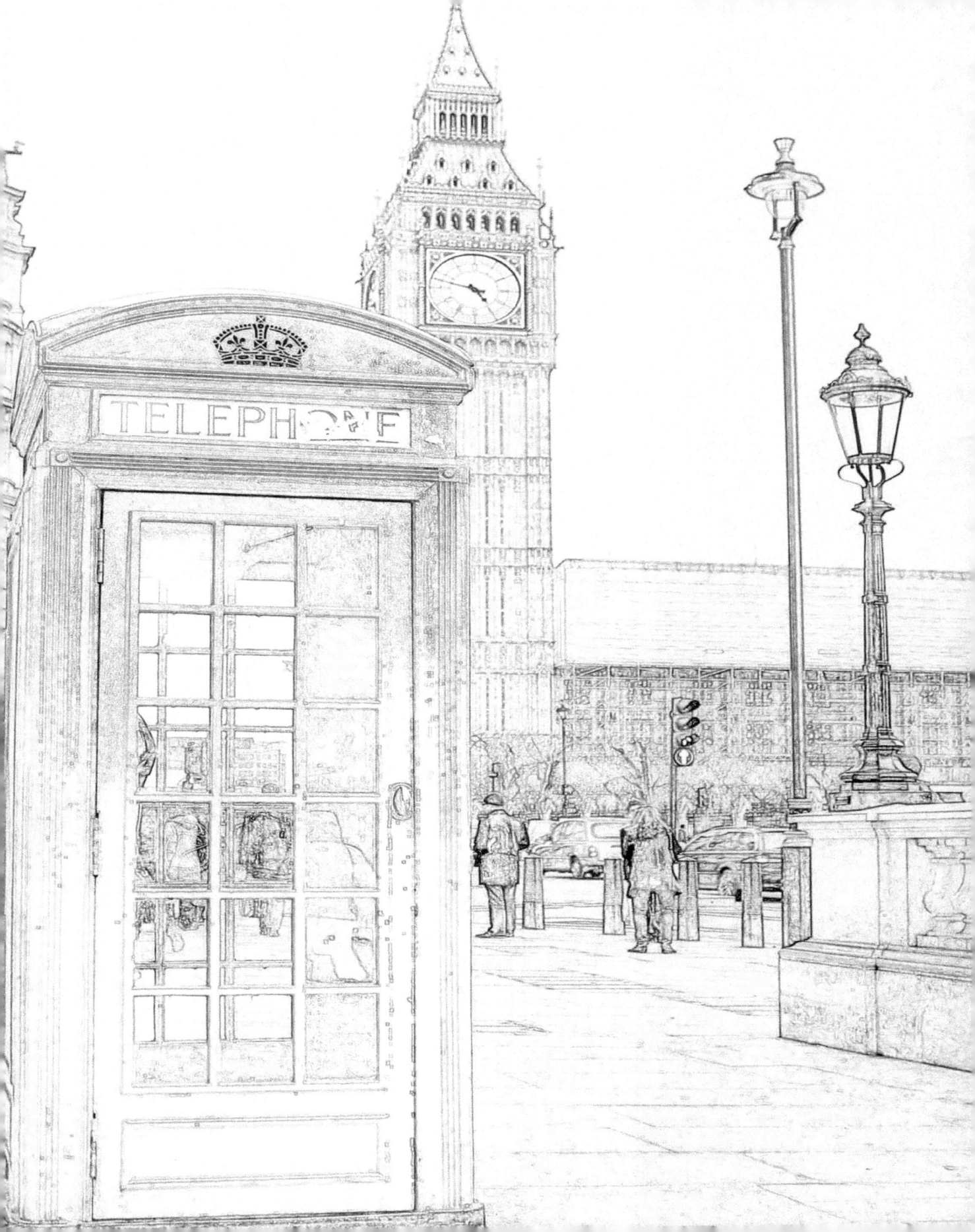

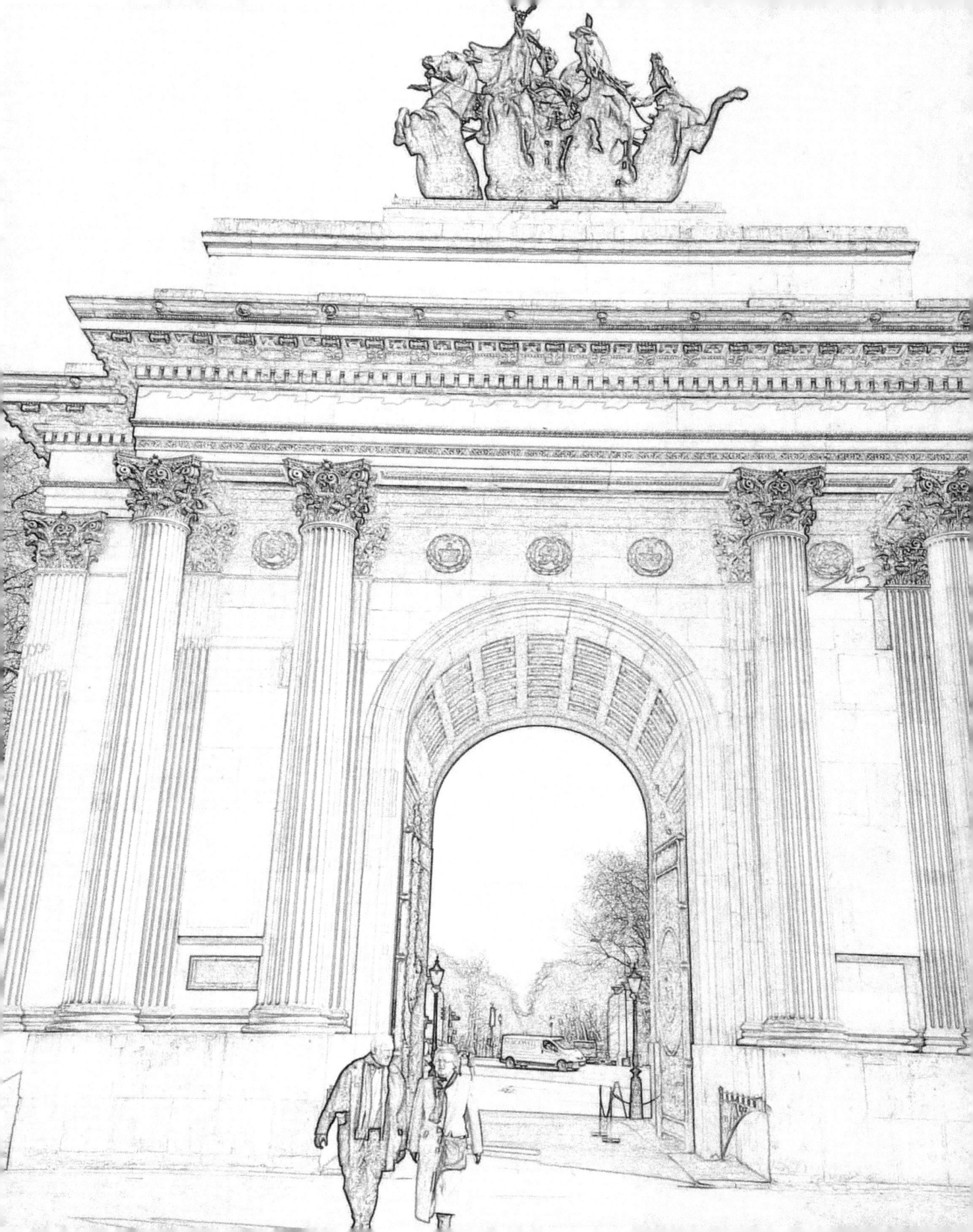

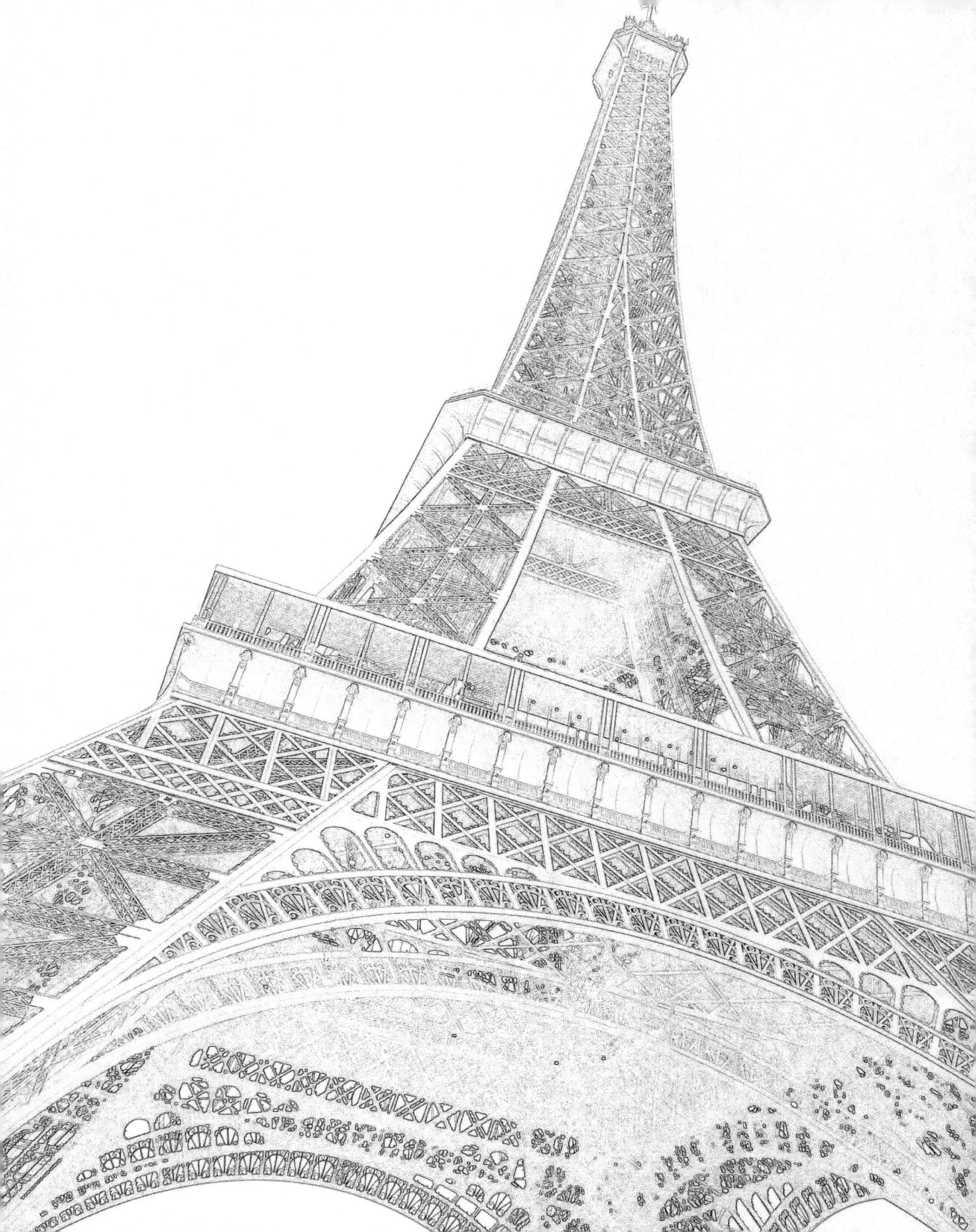

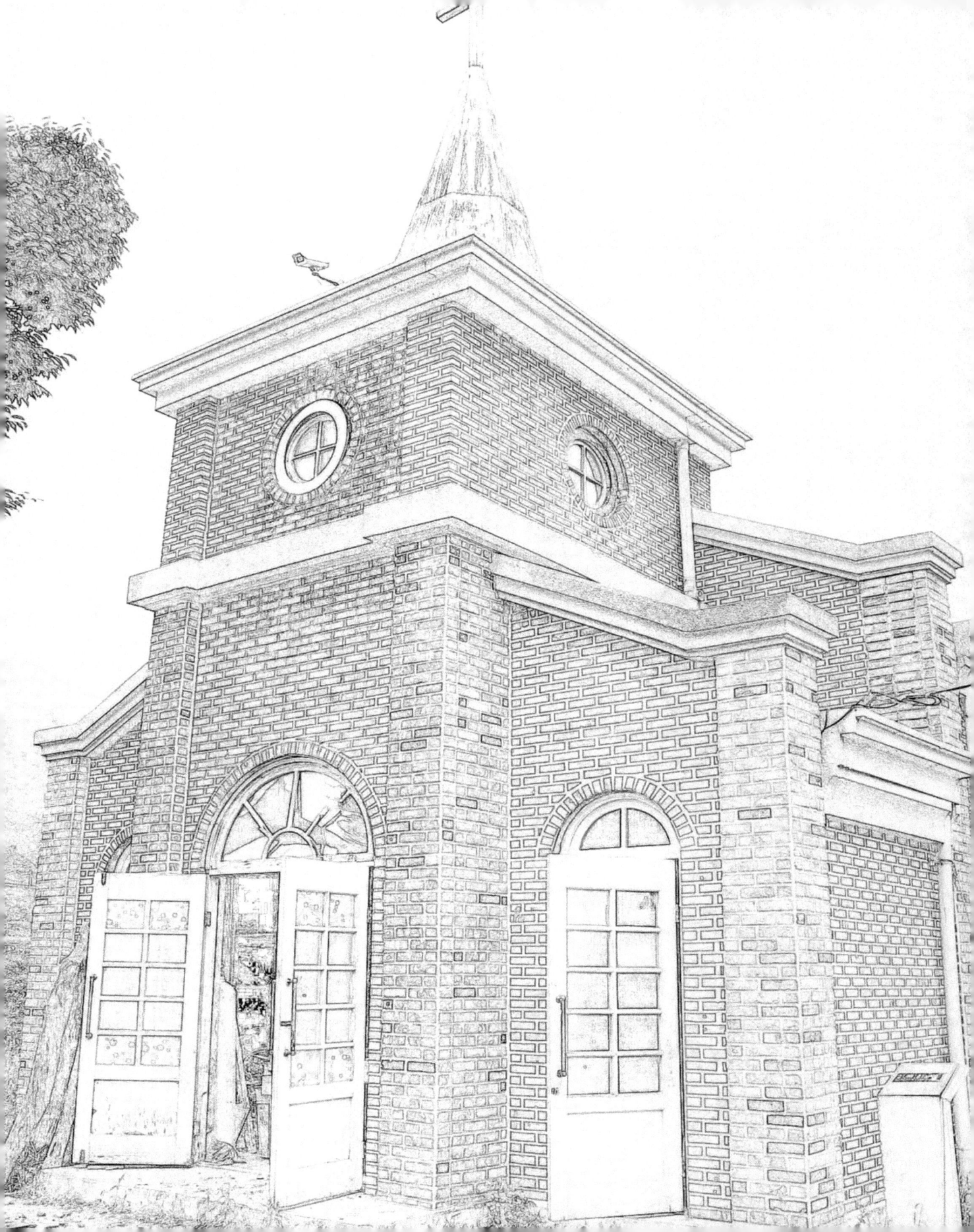

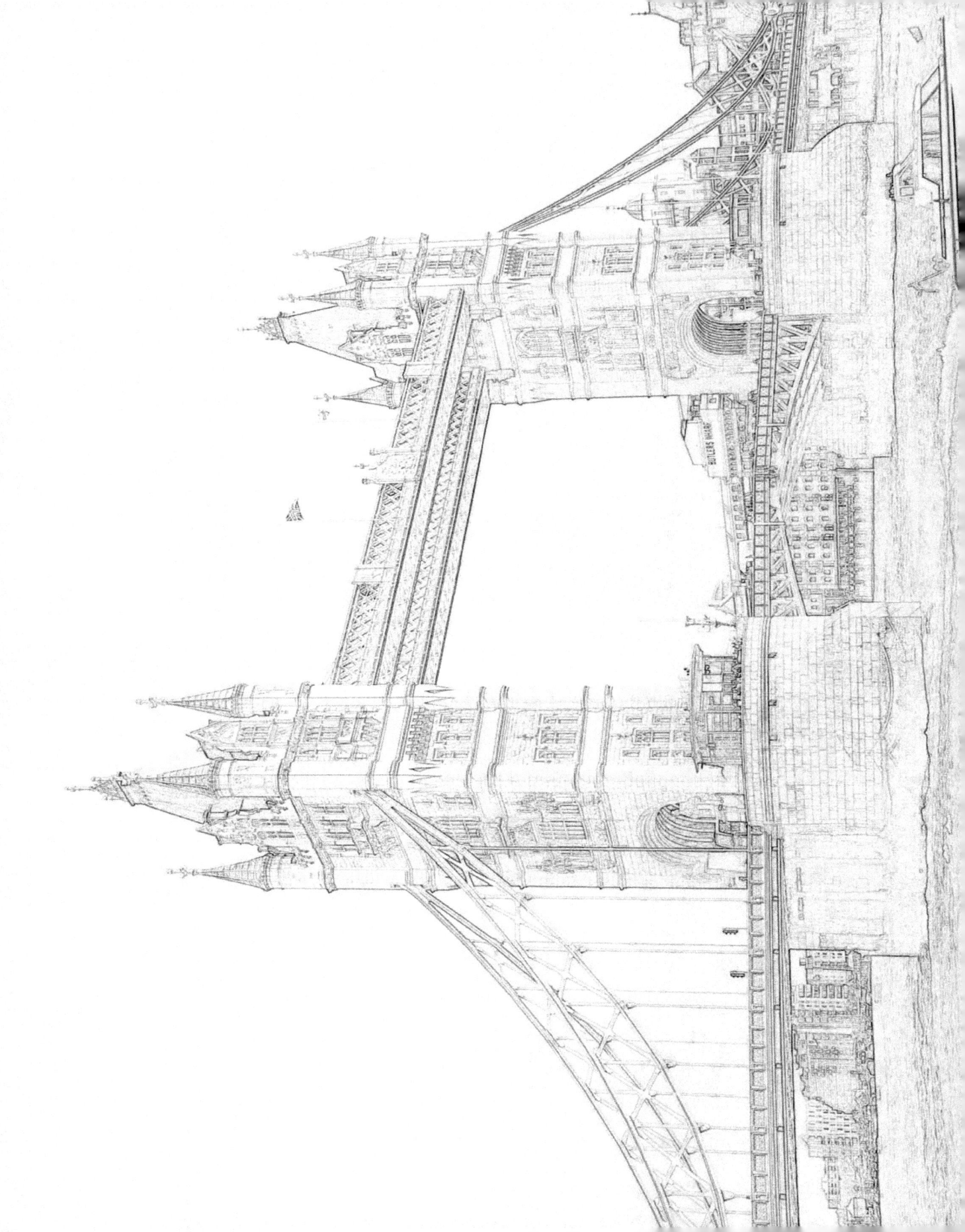

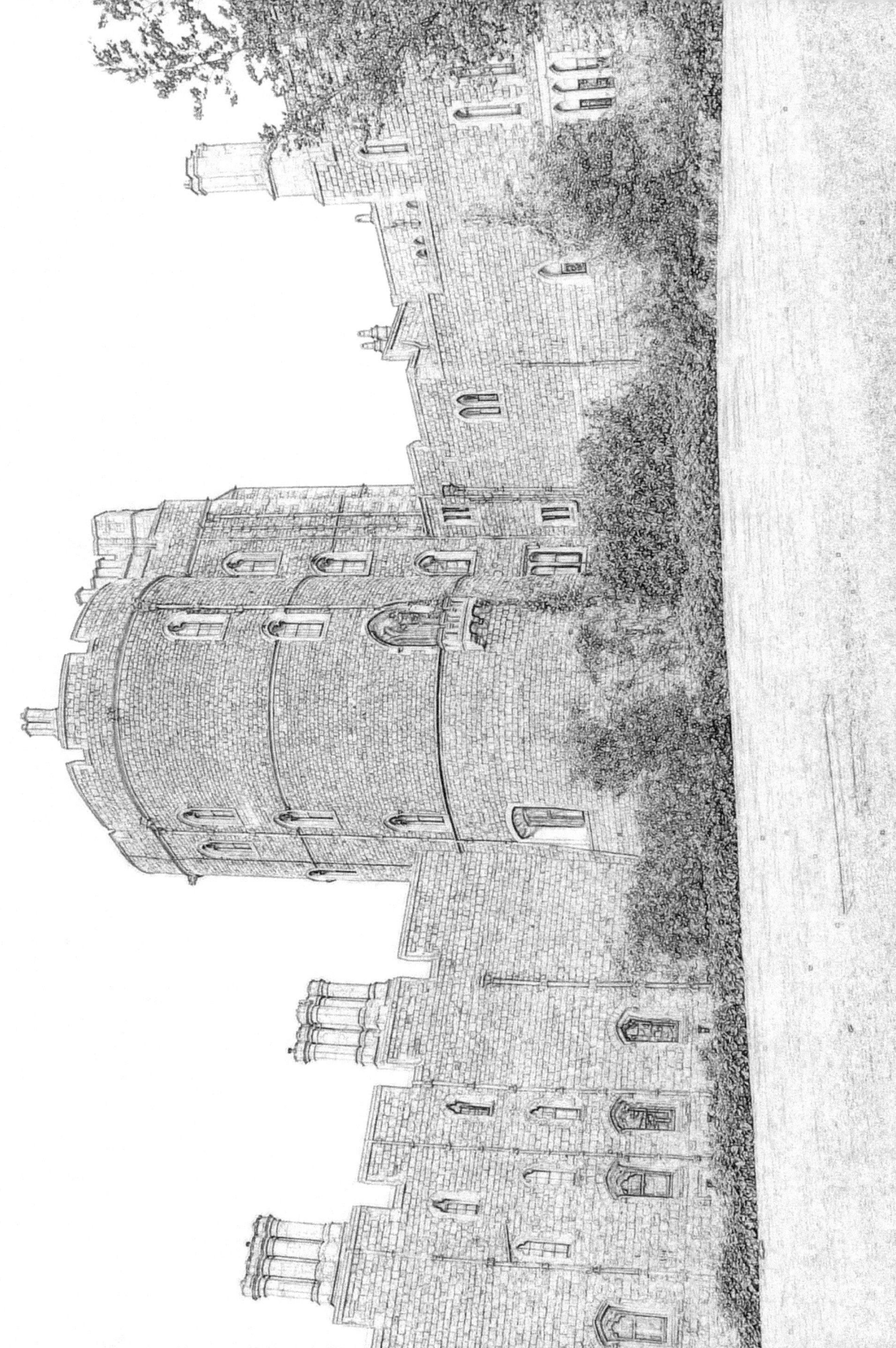

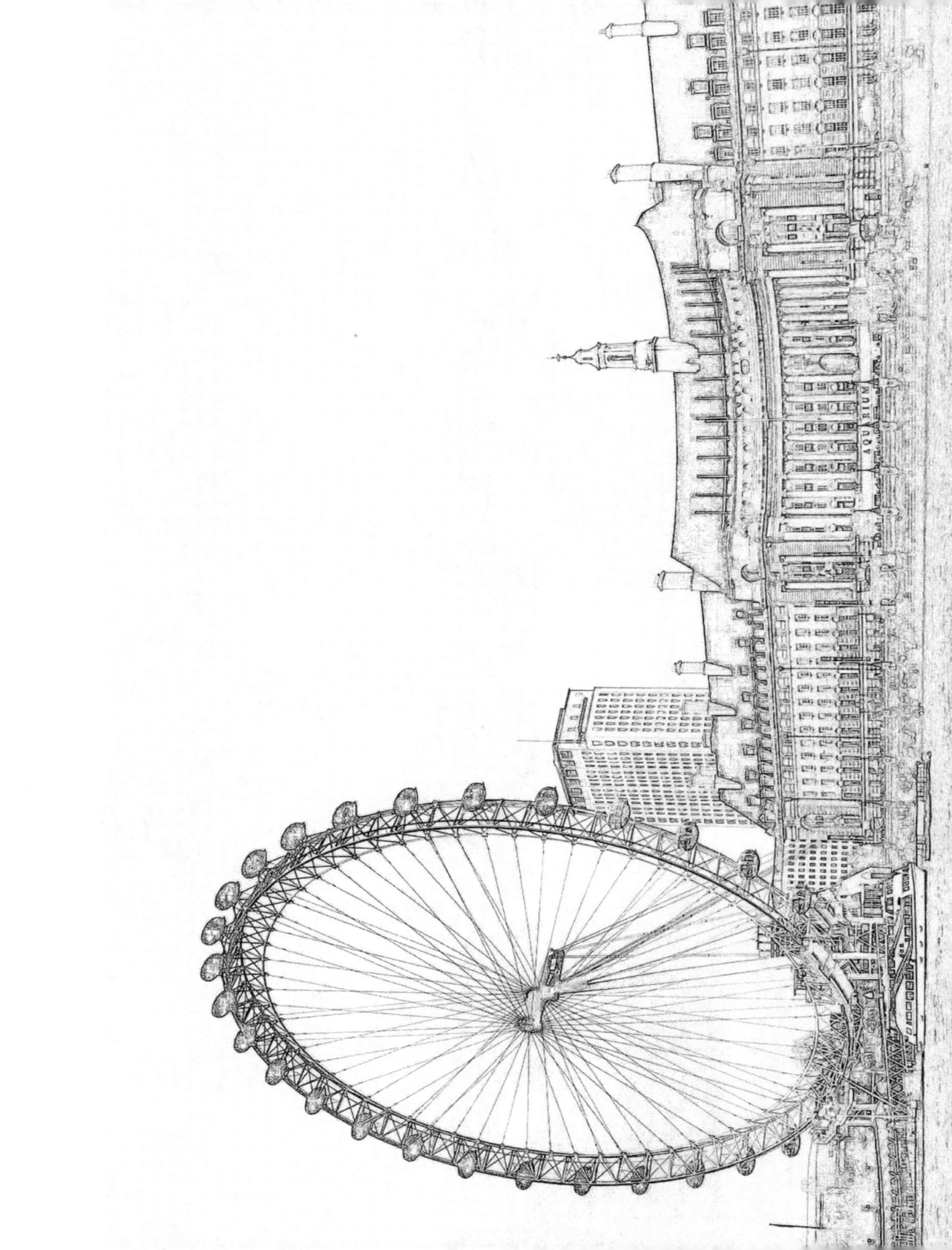

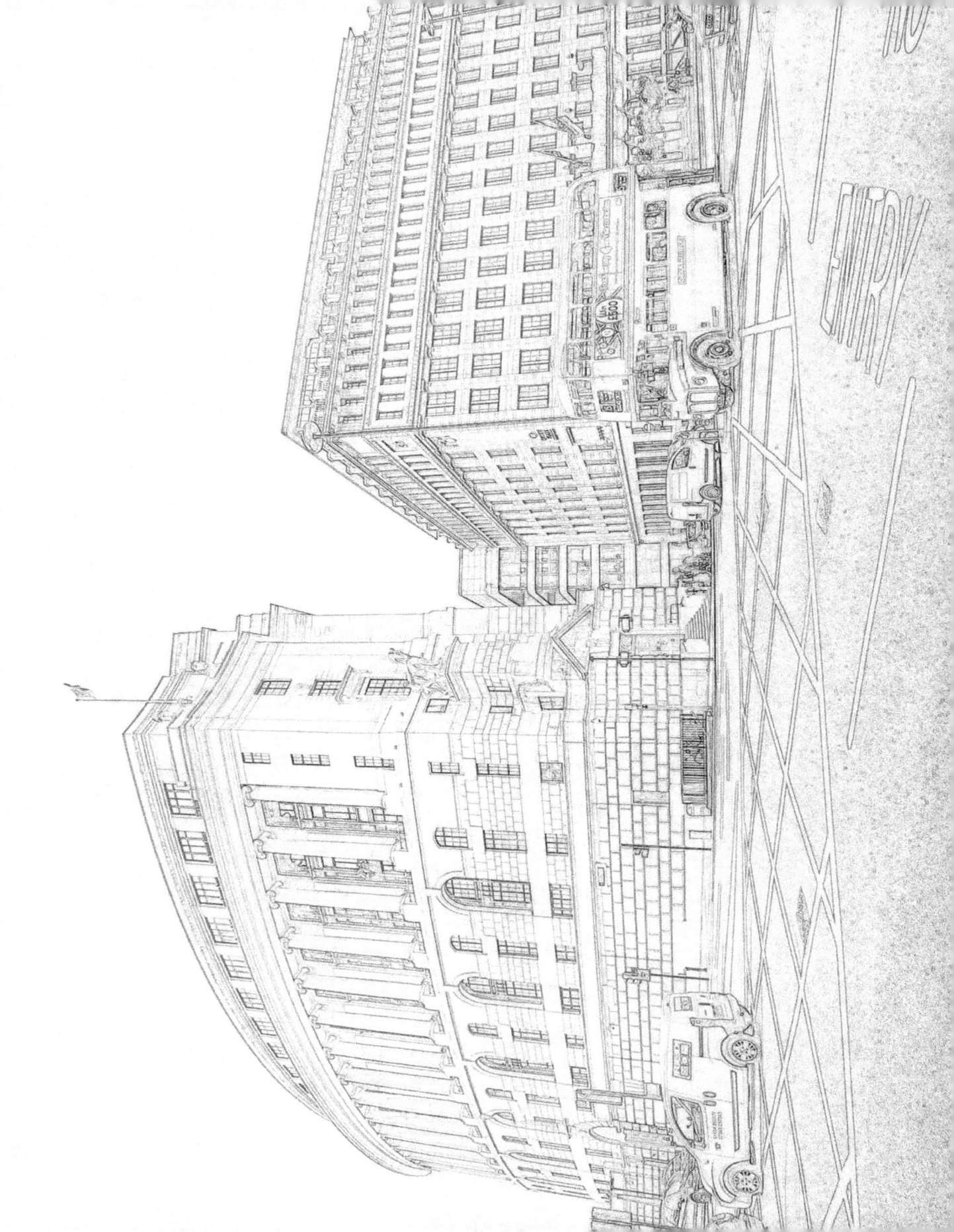

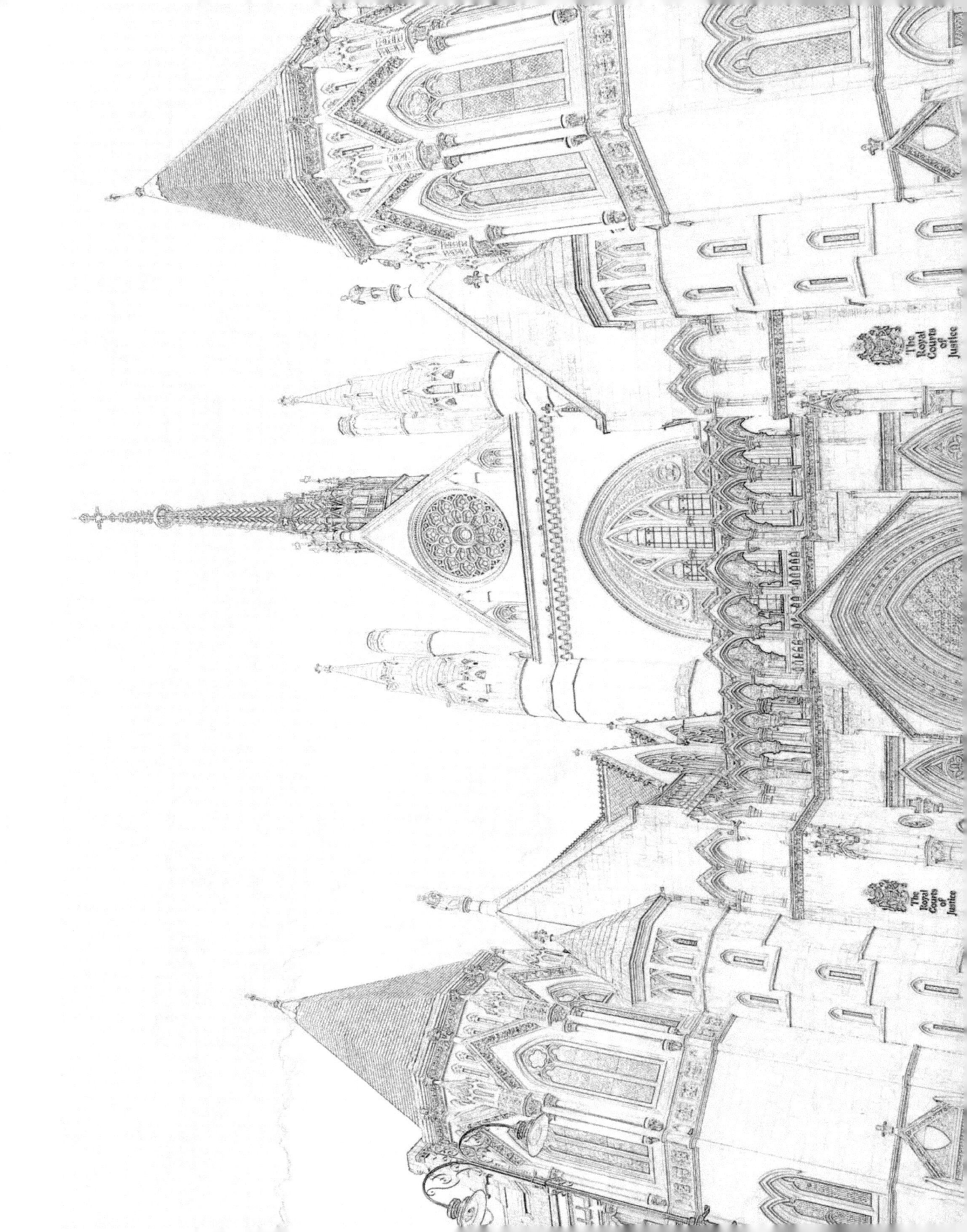

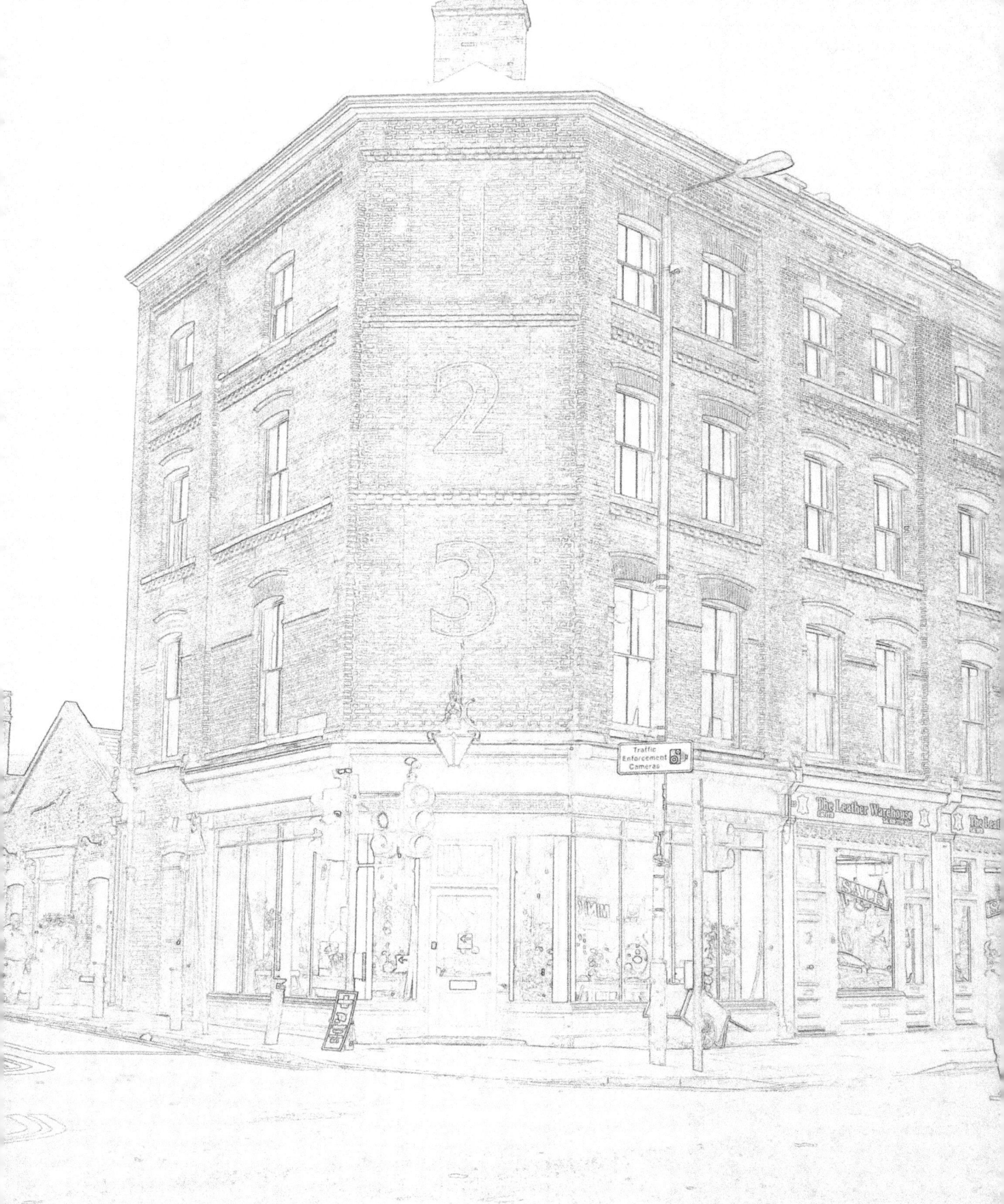

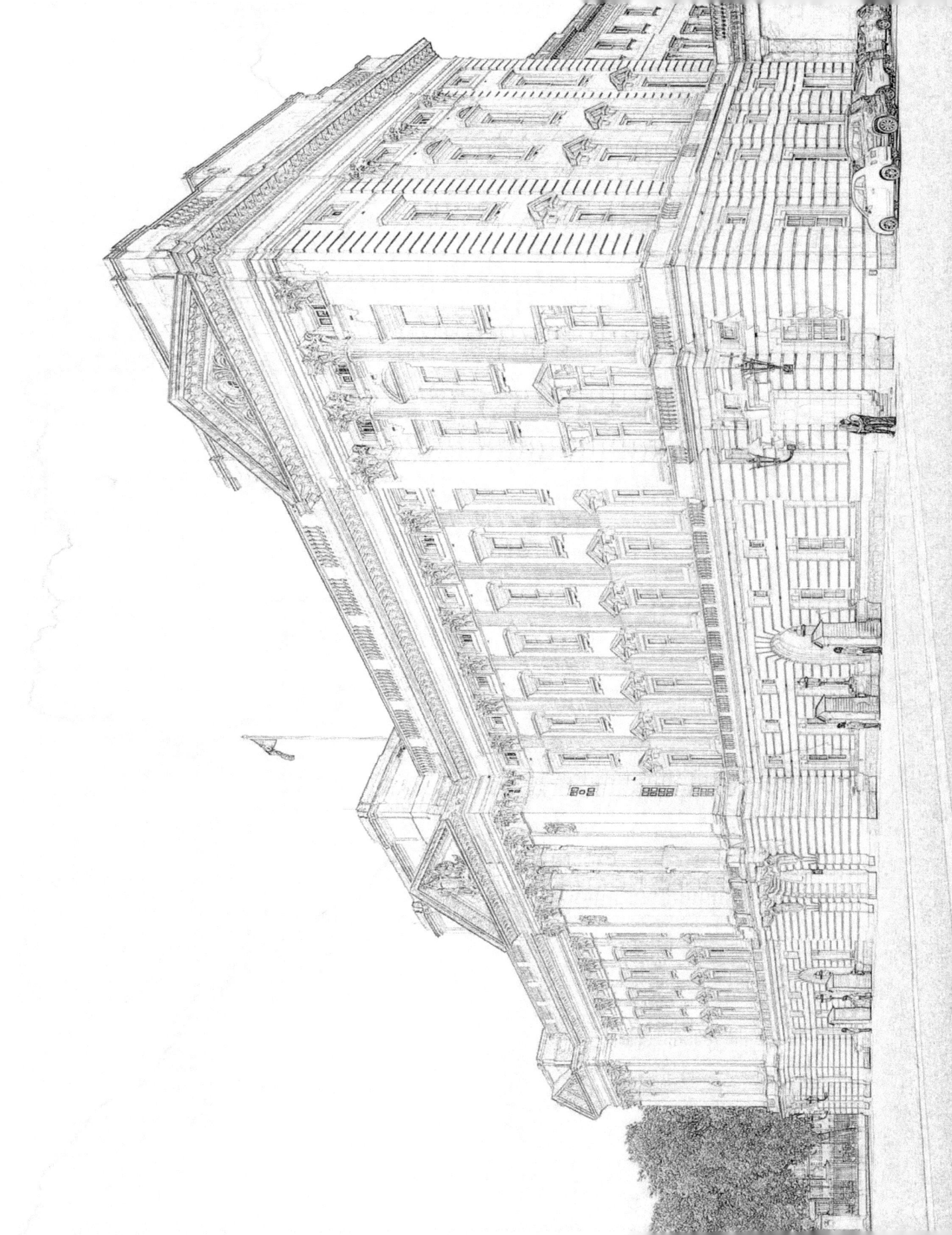

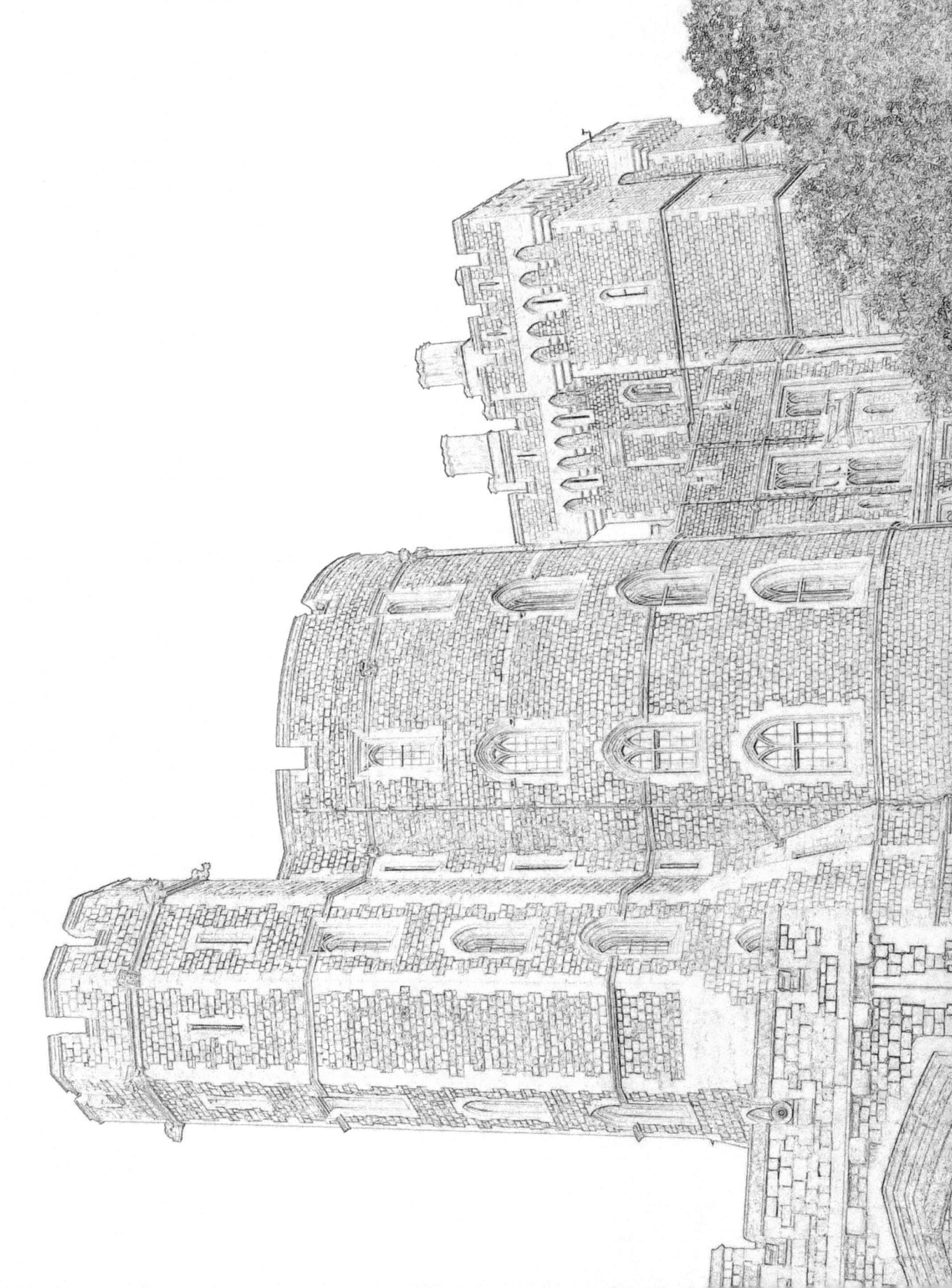

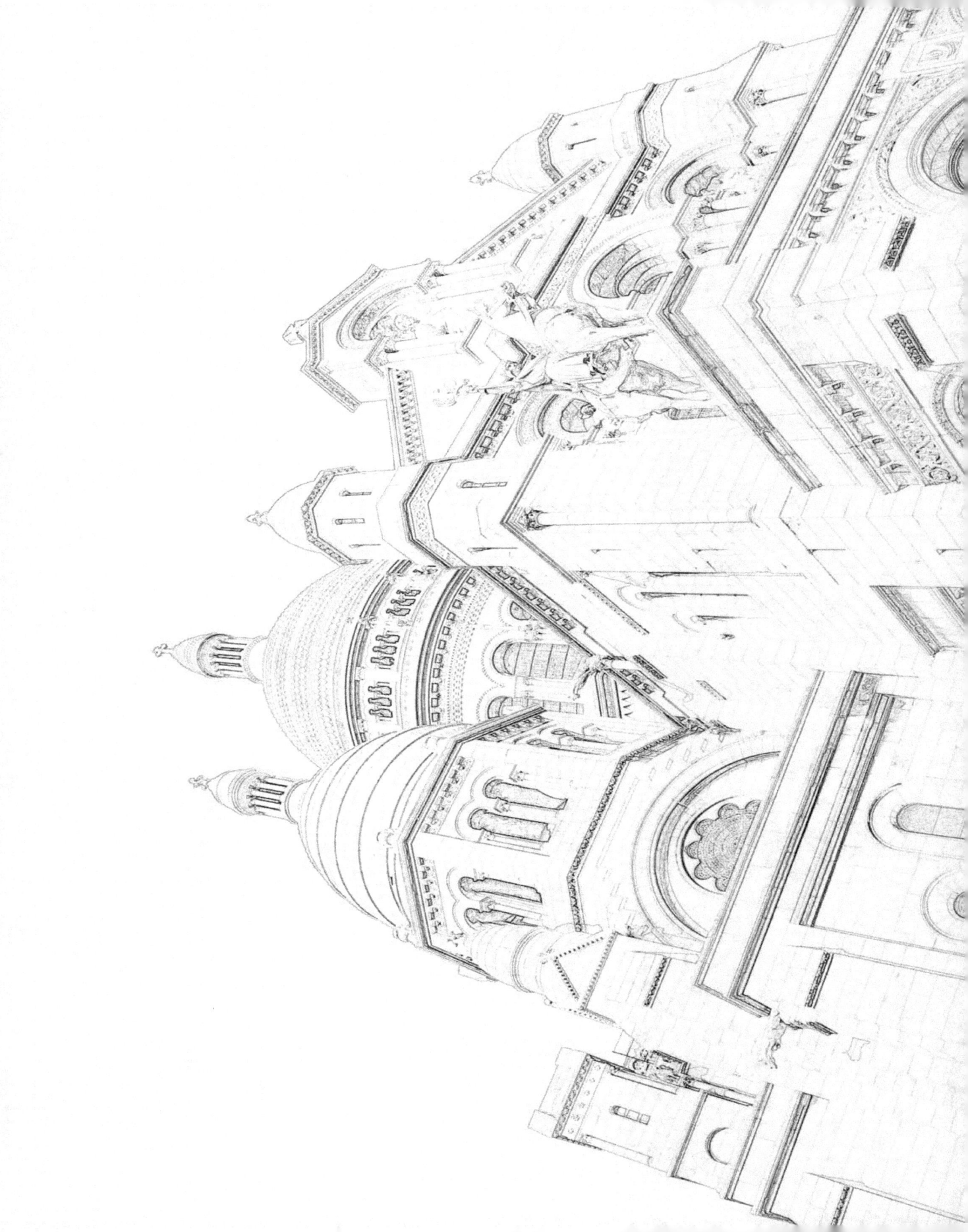

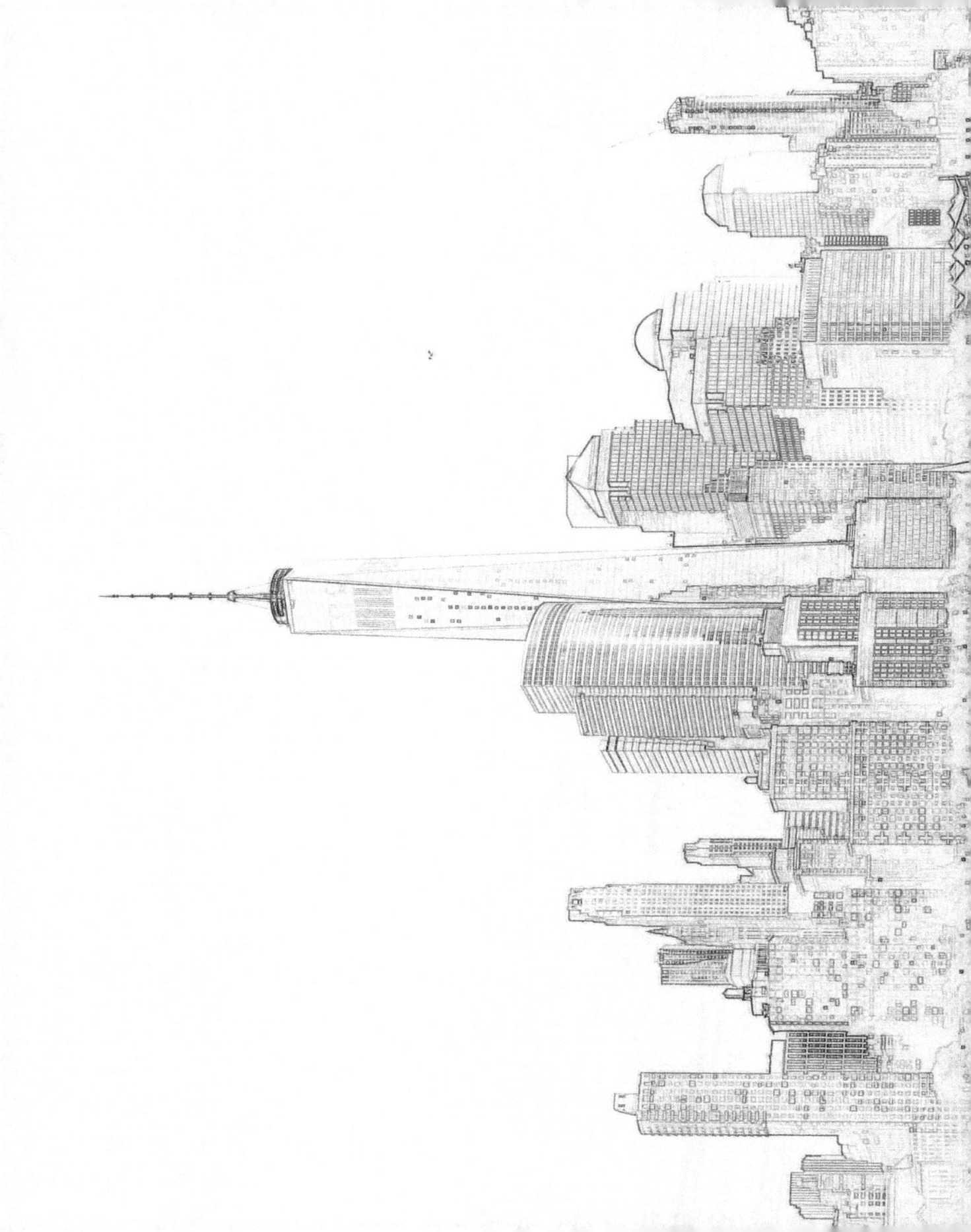

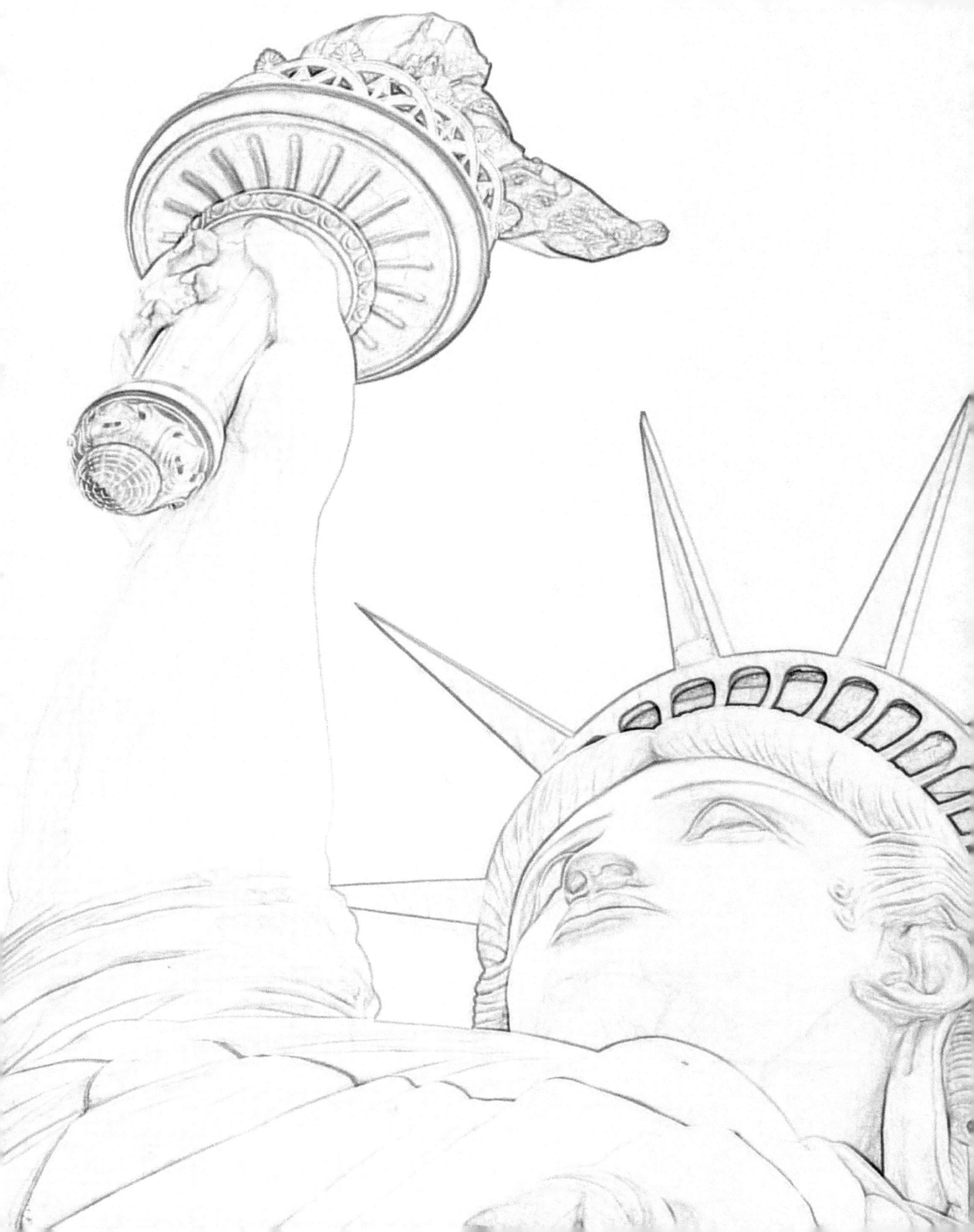

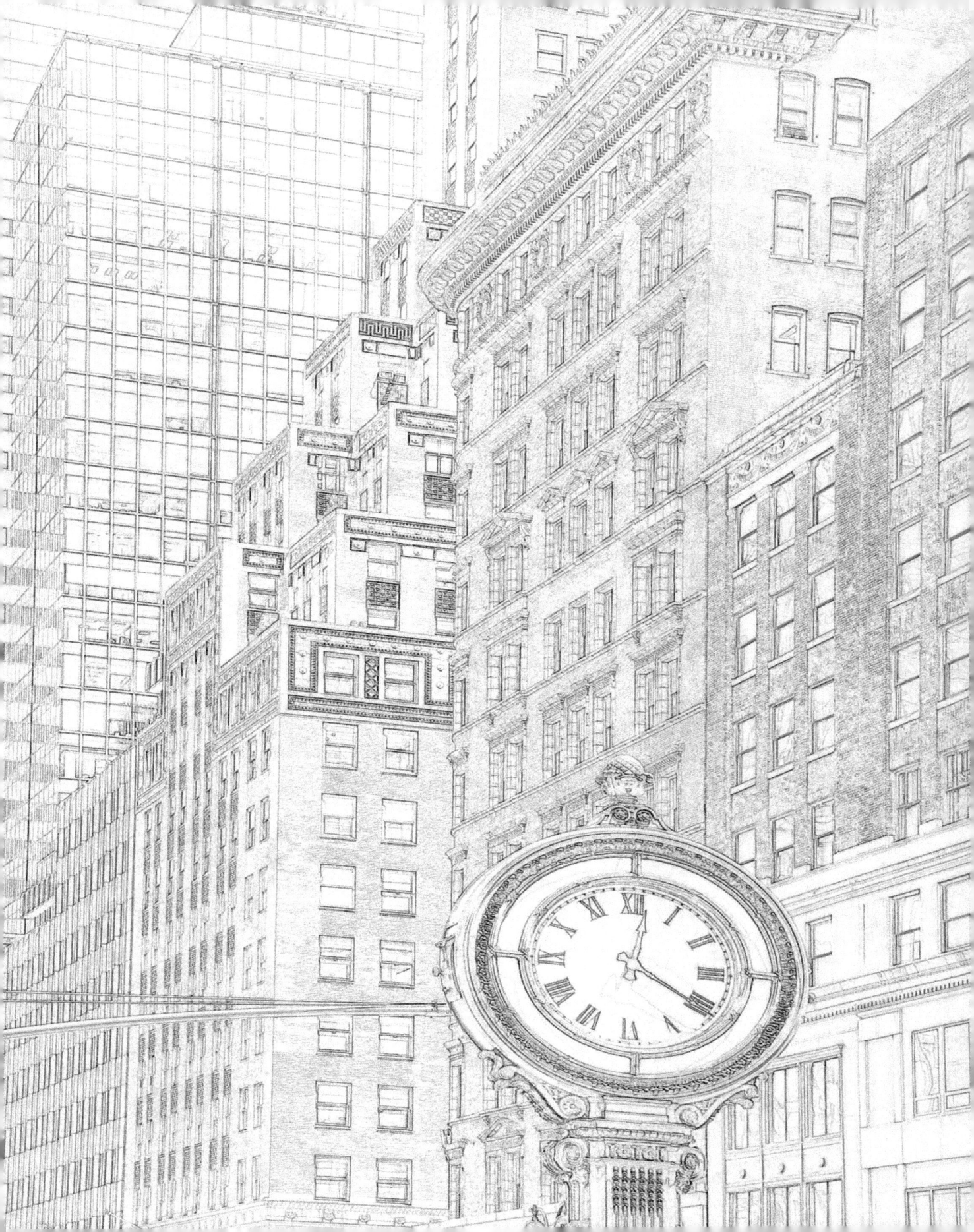

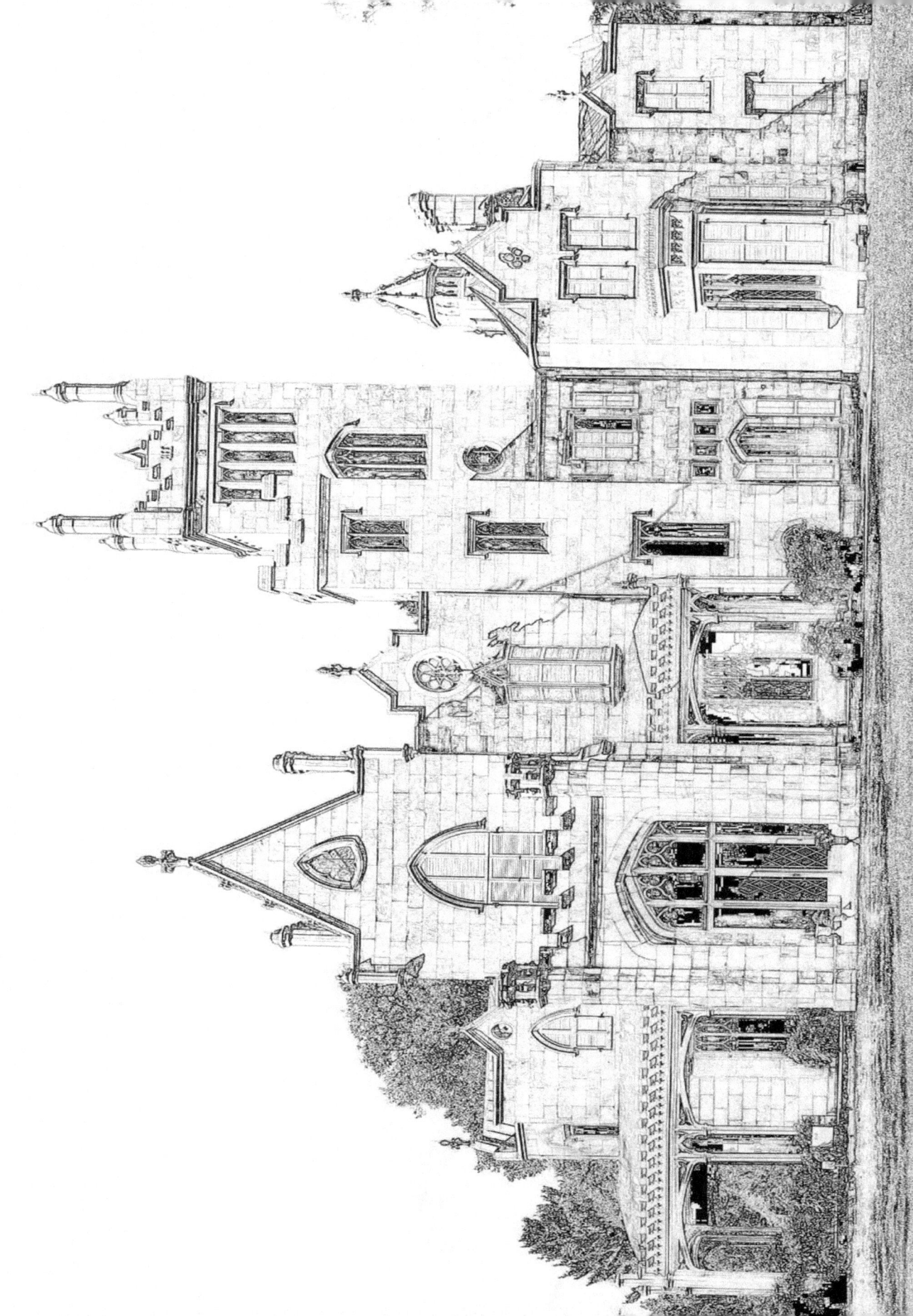

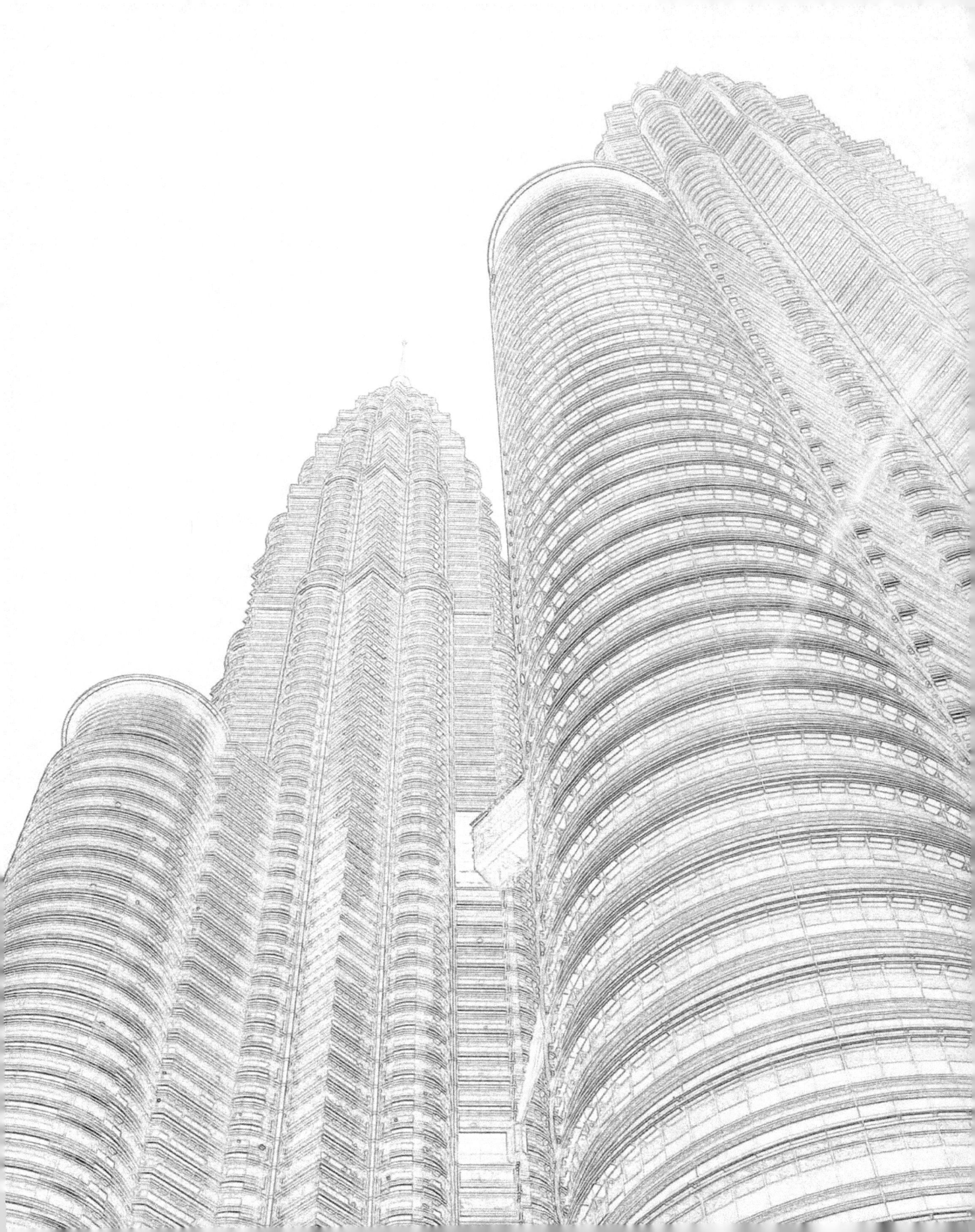

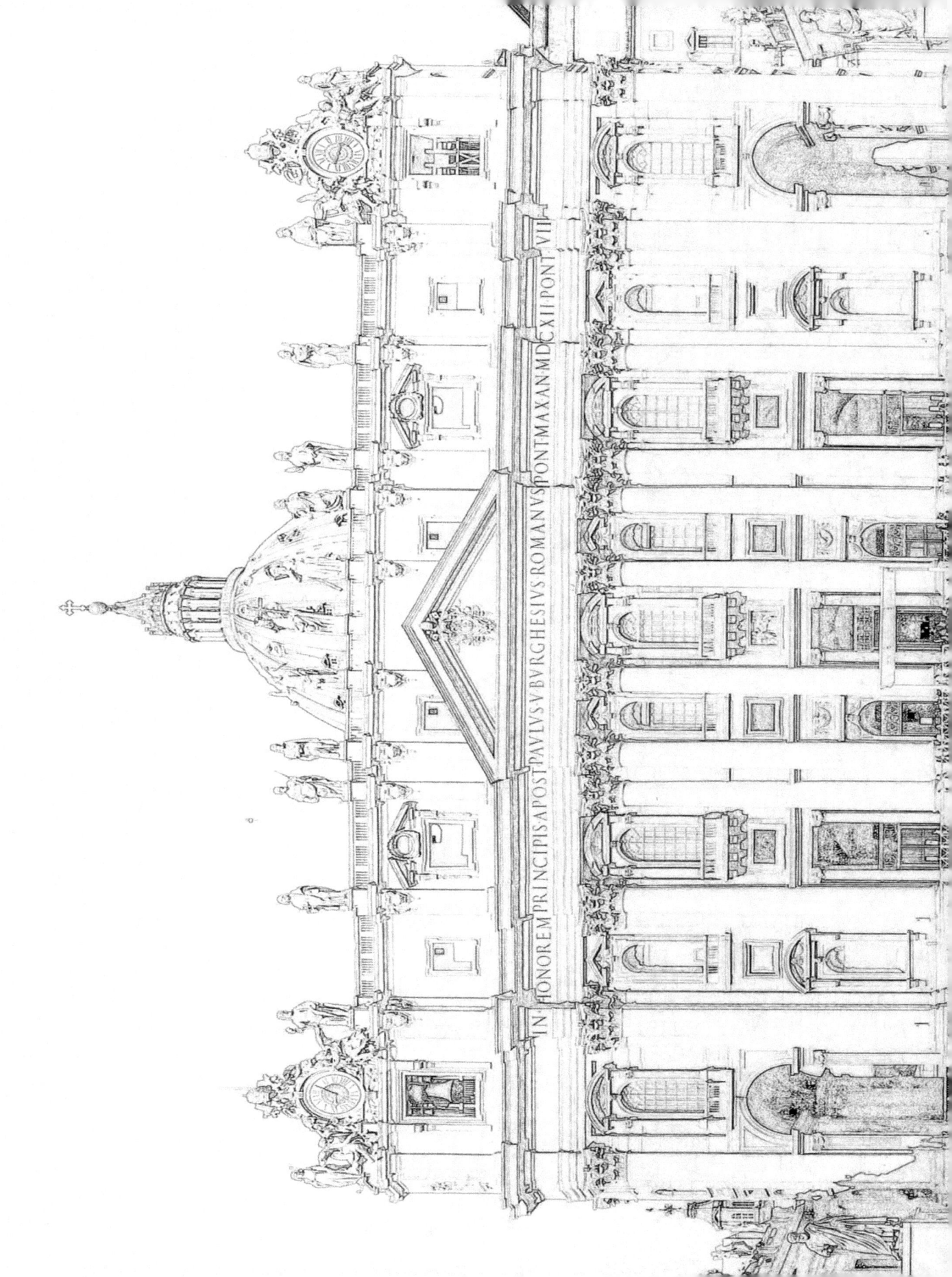

IN·HONOREM·PRINCIPIS·APOST·PAVLVS·V·BVRGHESIVS·ROMANVS·PONT·MAX·AN·MDCXII·PONT·VII

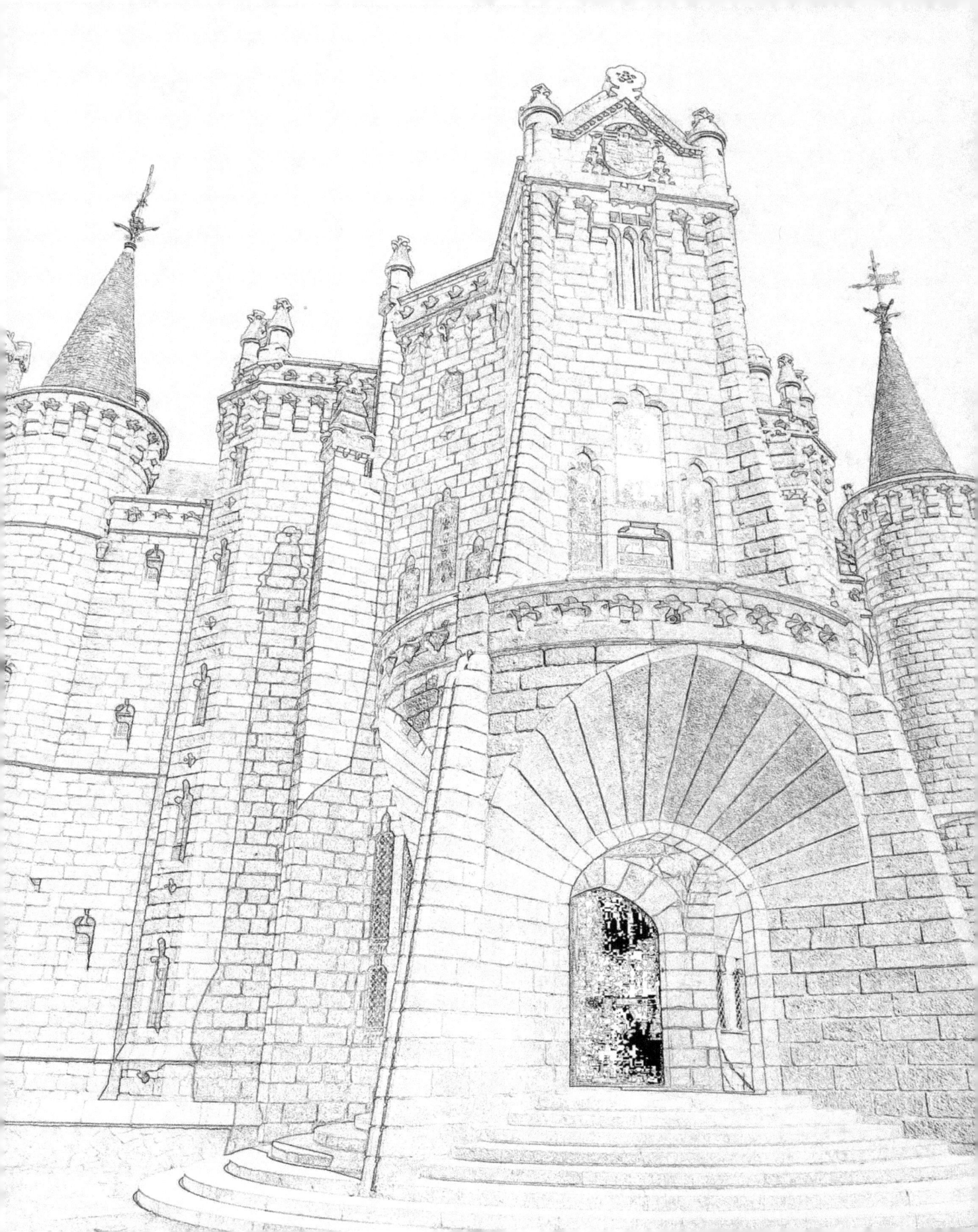

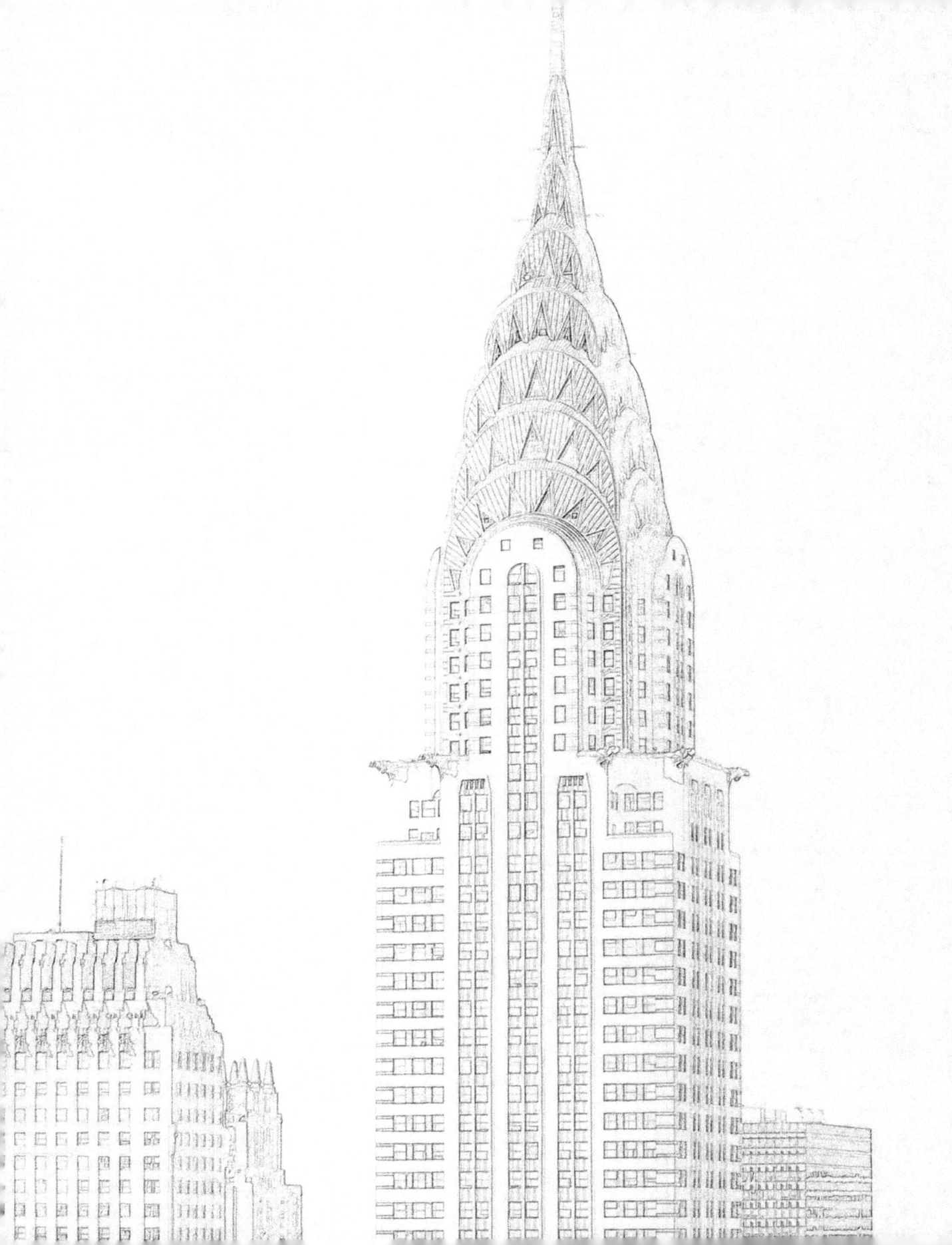

Thank you

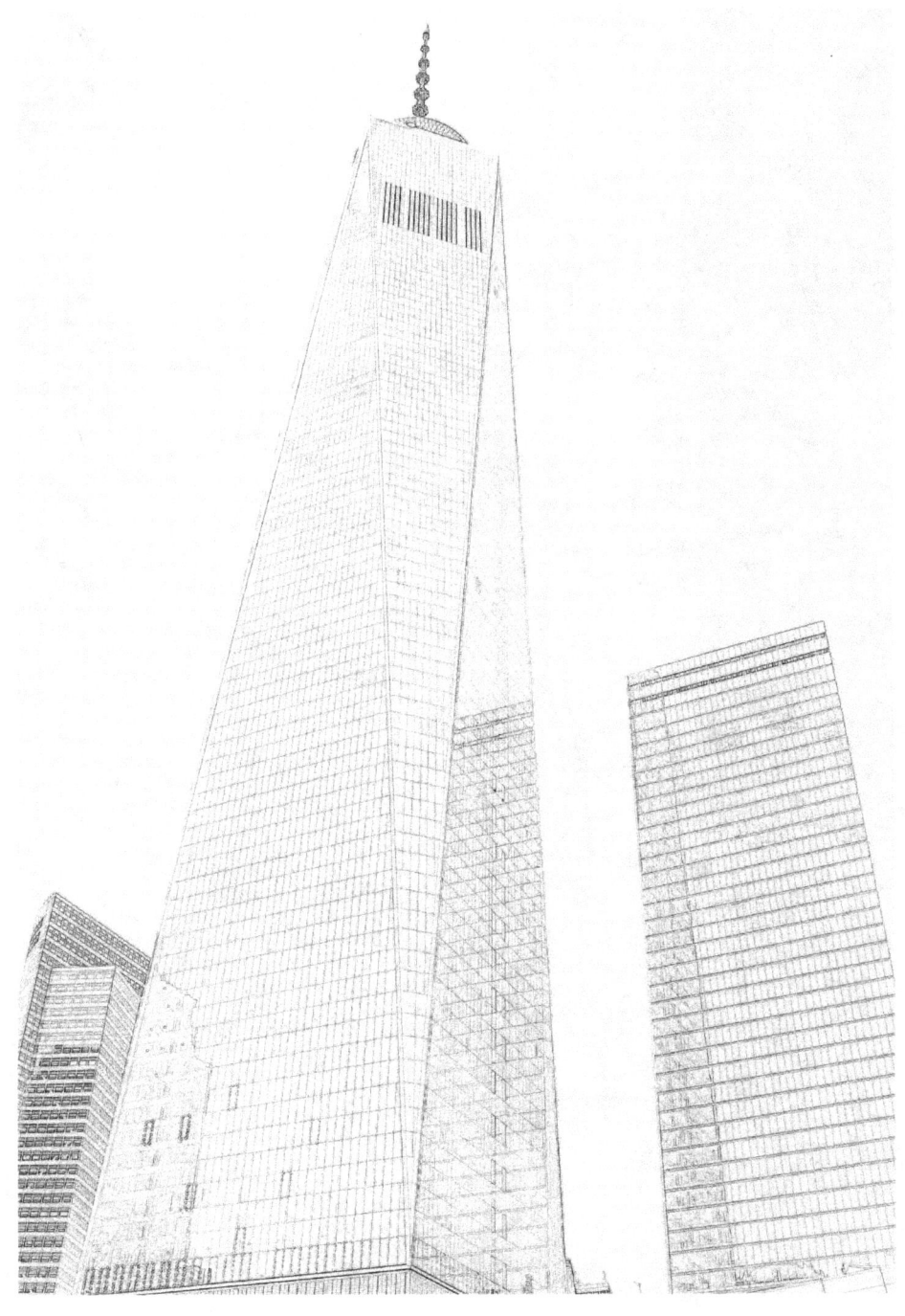